HIP-HOP INSIDER

HIP-HOP
GROUPS

By Rebecca Morris

CONTENT CONSULTANT
EVE ROBERTSON
YORK UNIVERSITY

Essential Library

An Imprint of Abdo Publishing | abdopublishing.com

Printed in the United States of America, North Mankato, Minnesota
042017
092017

THIS BOOK CONTAINS
RECYCLED MATERIALS

Cover Photo: Reed Saxon/AP Images
Interior Photos: Stuart Ramson/AP Images, 5; Seth Wenig/AP Images, 6, 8; David Corio/Michael Ochs Archives/Getty Images, 9; Ed Bailey/AP Images, 14; Ilya S. Savenok/Getty Images Entertainment/Getty Images, 17; Michael Ochs Archives/ Getty Images, 19; Al Pereira/Michael Ochs Archives/Getty Images, 21; Andy Sturmey/Photoshot/Newscom, 23; Gary Gershoff/MediaPunch/IPX/AP Images, 25; Mirrorpix/Newscom, 26–27, 32–33; Daily Record/Mirrorpix/Newscom, 31; Nigel Wright/Mirrorpix/Newscom, 36; Everett Collection, 39, 47; Bebeto Mathews/AP Images, 41; Charles Sykes/Invision/AP Images, 43; Pymca/UIG/Universal Images Group/Newscom, 45; Sean Thorton/JG3/ZJE Wenn Photos/Newscom, 48; Paul A. Hebert/Invision/AP Images, 52–53; Karl Grant/Retna/Photoshot/Newscom, 57; Matt Sayles/Invision/AP Images, 59; MediaPunch/Rex Features/AP Images, 62–63; Jim Cooper/AP Images, 66; Jason Kempin/FilmMagic/Getty Images, 69; Mark J. Terrill/AP Images, 70–71; PYMCAUIG Universal Images Group/Newscom, 75; Robb D. Cohen/Invision/AP Images, 77; Paul Hurschmann/AP Images, 79; Ron Frehm/ AP Images, 81; Chance Yeh/Patrick McMullan/Getty Images, 83; Johnny Nunez/ WireImage/Getty Images, 87; Catherine McGann/Archive Photos/Getty Images, 89; J. Stone/Shutterstock Images, 91; Charles Sykes/AP Images, 94–95

Editor: Jenna Trnka
Series Designer: Jake Nordby

Publisher's Cataloging-in-Publication Data
Names: Morris, Rebecca, author.
Title: Hip-hop groups / by Rebecca Morris.
Description: Minneapolis, MN : Abdo Publishing, 2018. | Series: Hip-hop insider |
    Includes bibliographical references and index.
Identifiers: LCCN 2016962251 | ISBN 9781532110290 (lib. bdg.) |
    ISBN 9781680788143 (ebook)
Subjects: LCSH: Hip-hop--Juvenile literature. | Group identity--Juvenile literature.
Classification: DDC 305--dc23
LC record available at http://lccn.loc.gov/2016962251

CONTENTS

1 HIP-HOP IN THE HALL OF FAME

At the 2007 Rock & Roll Hall of Fame induction ceremony, Grandmaster Flash and the Furious Five burst onto the stage to accept their honor. Wearing oversized jackets, gold chains, and baggy T-shirts and pants, they waved to the crowd and nodded their heads to the beat of their own music playing in the background. Members of the group stepped up to the microphone to thank the people who had helped them with their careers. As Grandmaster Flash took the microphone to wrap up the speeches, he gave a loud shout-out to "every break dancer, every graffiti artist, every MC, every DJ," saying, "We here!"[1] The crowd cheered as he thrust his fist in the air. When Grandmaster Flash said "here," he wasn't

Grandmaster Flash pioneered hip-hop, experimenting with new deejaying styles.

referring simply to the physical location where he stood, the Waldorf Astoria Hotel in New York. Instead, he was referring to a pivotal moment—his hip-hop group's induction into the Rock & Roll Hall of Fame. It was the first time a hip-hop group had received that honor. As Jay Z put it in his introduction at the ceremony, "Ladies and gentlemen, you're witnessing history."[2]

Jay Z, another hip-hop star, had the honor of introducing Grandmaster Flash and the Furious Five at the induction ceremony.

Established in 1983, the Rock & Roll Hall of Fame recognizes artists for "unquestionable musical excellence and talent" who "have had a significant impact on the development, evolution, and preservation" of music.[3] In addition, artists can only be inducted if at least 25 years have passed since the release of their first album. Therefore, Grandmaster Flash and the Furious Five's induction was not only a sign of the members' exceptional work but also that they had made a lasting mark in the world of music. In their case, that mark came both in the style and content of their music. That is, the group was innovative in the techniques and technologies it popularized as well as with its lyrics.

Formed in the Bronx

Grandmaster Flash and the Furious Five officially formed in the South Bronx of New York City in 1976. At the time, Grandmaster Flash, whose real name is Joseph Saddler,

Grandmaster Flash and the Furious Five receive a standing ovation at the 2007 Hall of Fame induction ceremony.

was a DJ known on the local rap scene for his creativity. He was unique because he treated the turntable, the crossfader, and other electronic equipment as musical instruments that could be played to create new sounds. These experiments were precursors to the electro-funk ingenuity on display in the group's recorded songs, such as "Scorpio" (1982), which music critic Mark Richardson praised as "the greatest early electro track and the best robot-rap of all time."[4] Meanwhile, Keef Cowboy (Robert Keith Wiggins), Melle Mel (Melvin Glover), the Kidd Creole

(Nathaniel Glover Jr.), Mr. Ness/Scorpio (Eddie Morris), and Rahiem (Guy Todd Williams) were building their reputations as rappers, MCs, and lyricists. During their first three years as a group, Grandmaster Flash and the

Grandmaster Flash performing in 1980

THE FURIOUS FALLING OUT

Like many hip-hop groups, Grandmaster Flash and the Furious Five went through some changes in its members. The group split in the mid-1980s because of disagreements over contracts and payments. Melle Mel, Cowboy, and Mr. Ness/Scorpio stuck together and released their own album, *Grandmaster Melle Mel and the Furious Five* (1984). Meanwhile, Grandmaster Flash continued working with Rahiem and the Kidd Creole, along with new group members, to produce additional albums. The original members got back together for a brief time in the late 1980s. Since then, various members have performed together for different projects and events.

Furious Five performed live shows throughout the clubs, parks, and streets of New York, highlighting their music as a dynamic and interactive art form. These shows featured exchanges between the DJ and the MCs, as well as passes in which the MCs would rhyme in unison. They also included call-and-response rhymes to involve the audience.

Message Rap

The group's developments in technology and technique evolved hip-hop's stylistic possibilities and remain staples in contemporary tracks; however, what drew increased attention to Grandmaster Flash and the Furious Five was their combination of those new approaches, along with their conscious lyricism. Conscious lyricism is also called lyrical social commentary, conscious hip-hop, and message rap. These are terms used to describe music that directly addresses social, cultural, political, racial, or economic injustices. In 1982, Grandmaster Flash and the Furious Five released "The Message," one of the most influential songs in establishing conscious lyricism as a component of hip-hop culture.

"The Message" gives a harsh portrait of inner-city life, focusing on poverty, hopelessness, and violence. Written at a time when the South Bronx faced serious problems, the song features many now-famous lines to express feelings of chaos and desperation. For example, the song opens by comparing the inner city to a jungle: "It's like a jungle sometimes, it makes me wonder how I keep from goin' under." This comparison paints a picture of a lawless place where everyday survival involves a struggle for basic necessities, such as food, shelter, and utilities. Later, the refrain

LIFE IN THE JUNGLE

The 1970s and 1980s were a particularly dark time for minority neighborhoods in the inner city of New York. Many businesses had closed and abandoned the areas. The government failed to enforce policies that would improve life, and policing practices were more harmful than helpful. "The Message" uses strong images to evoke these conditions through the five senses. It names the sounds of breaking glass, the smell of urine, the sight of rats and roaches, the taste of garbage, and the feel of air from cars rushing by front stoops and broken windows.

repeats, "Don't push me, 'cause I'm close to the edge / I'm trying not to lose my head." According to these lines, the inner-city jungle can be so taxing that many people teeter close to their breaking points. In fact, the song's speaker does eventually break. With no education, no decent job prospects, and no hope for the future, his life descends into a spiral of crime, sexual violence, imprisonment, and finally suicide.

The Message of "The Message"

The content of "The Message" is grim but important because it provides an unfiltered glimpse into the lives of people whose struggles—as a result of social, political, economic, racial, and cultural injustices—were largely ignored. The six members of Grandmaster Flash and the Furious Five experienced these overlooked struggles firsthand. Grandmaster Flash, for instance, remembers the desperate rioting that occurred when a major blackout struck New York in July 1977. Even though Flash has also said he is grateful for his Bronx upbringing, moments such as those July riots stuck with him and other members of the group. Furthermore, the group members proved hip-hop music could be an outlet for their feelings. Many academics and cultural commentators have noted that through their efforts, Grandmaster Flash and the Furious

Five "gave voice to the voiceless."[5]

Not only did songs such as "The Message" lend a voice to those who needed one, but the success of the group also began carving out new avenues for inner-city artists who might otherwise have felt limited. The song inspired other artists, such as Jay Z. Given the importance of the cultural message in "The Message," it is fitting that the crowd rapped along to its refrain at the group's historic Rock & Roll Hall of Fame induction. The diverse crowd's ability to recall the lyrics and rhyme from memory made a powerful statement. It was a testament to how hip-hop had

THE BLACKOUT OF 1977

New York's infamous 1977 blackout occurred during a major heat wave in July. The city's energy systems were straining to keep up with the extra demand for electricity to cool buildings. When a lightning strike hit a generator, there was an even greater burden on the systems. The poor infrastructure, bad official planning, and employee mistakes during the emergency resulted in a major loss of power for millions. In economically depressed areas of the city, people turned to looting and rioting. Even before the blackout, looting was already a big problem in minority neighborhoods. Frustrated citizens robbed many stores and abandoned housing buildings. This blackout only stirred the tensions further and provided increased opportunities for looters. As more people filled the streets, rioting broke out.

The riots during the 1977 blackout caused extensive damage in New York.

engraved its innovative styles and conscious content onto mainstream awareness.

Power in Numbers

Grandmaster Flash and the Furious Five's work showed that collaborating with other artists, sampling from previous songs, borrowing from musical influences, and interacting with crews and audiences were and still are important features of hip-hop. It is no surprise groups have occupied a special place in hip-hop history and have developed from their early beginnings in the 1970s to the supergroups common in the twenty-first century.

> "Thirty years later, rappers have become rock stars, movie stars, leaders, educators, philanthropists, even CEOs. But none of this would be possible without the work of the men [in Grandmaster Flash and the Furious Five]."[6]
>
> —Jay Z

2 PIONEERING GROUPS

When DJs, MCs, and rappers began performing hip-hop in the 1970s, it was very much a live art form. Artists performed their acts at house parties, in public parks, and on the streets at block parties. These acts could last hours as the artists delivered a steady stream of rhymes. That kind of performance engaged audiences because it allowed them to interact with the artists and the music for extended periods of time. However, it also meant hip-hop's reach was limited to those who heard the live performances. It seemed nearly impossible to put such long musical acts on recorded albums that could be distributed across the nation.

The Sugarhill Gang is often regarded as the first hip-hop group to

Even if artists and producers could figure out how to record hip-hop for radio, it wasn't clear if mainstream audiences would relate to this type of music, since it was so heavily rooted in tight-knit minority communities.

THE MOTHER OF HIP-HOP

Sylvia Robinson was one of the most influential forces in bringing hip-hop into the mainstream, which was a noteworthy achievement because few women worked in music production at the time. Robinson began her career in music at the young age of 14. She went on to record several R&B hits in the 1950s with her singing partner, Mickey Baker. Robinson also achieved success as a solo artist, and she cofounded her first production company, All Platinum Records, with her husband, Joe Robinson. When that company was in financial trouble, Robinson found inspiration for a new venture while watching a hip-hop act at the Harlem World nightclub. She began Sugar Hill Records to promote hip-hop artists. The Sugarhill Gang was the label's first group.

Pioneering hip-hop groups in the late 1970s and early 1980s answered these questions. The first groups introduced hip-hop by connecting it to popular trends of the time, which then paved the way for hip-hop to settle into its own unique styles.

Breaking into Mainstream Music

In 1979, the Sugarhill Gang opened wide possibilities for hip-hop with its hit song "Rapper's Delight." The trio formed under the direction of producer Sylvia Robinson shortly before the release of its debut song. Robinson had the three—Wonder

Sylvia Robinson helped bring groups to the hip-hop industry.

Mike (Michael Wright), Big Bank Hank (Henry Jackson), and Master Gee (Guy O'Brien)—audition for her on a Friday evening. "Rapper's Delight" was recorded the following Monday. The full version of the song runs almost 15 minutes long, but there is also a shortened version approximately six minutes long. Even on the shortened track, recognizable elements of hip-hop take center stage. These elements include strong rap rhymes, handoffs between artists, call-and-response

HIP-HOP'S FIRST RECORDED SONG

Despite the important place "Rapper's Delight" holds in music history, scholars often point out it wasn't technically the first recorded hip-hop song. Two months before Sugar Hill Records released "Rapper's Delight," another label, Spring Records, released a party-rock hip-hop track by the Fatback Band. That song, "King Tim III," was a popular club song for a short time, and it even reached the number 26 spot on the R&B charts. However, because Spring Records didn't promote it much, the song was overshadowed by "Rapper's Delight."

passes, and self-reference to the artists and their material possessions.

The length of this short track was perfect for a radio release. The song also includes sampling from the disco hit "Good Times" by the group Chic. The shortened length and the sampling of a trendy, recognizable disco track made "Rapper's Delight" an ideal song to introduce people to hip-hop in a familiar way. Those strategies worked, and after the song was released in October 1979, it had a 12-week run on the *Billboard* pop charts.

Meeting Criticism

Despite the song's success in spreading hip-hop to new audiences and markets, the Sugarhill Gang's music was met with criticism from other hip-hop artists. Grandmaster Caz, a DJ, MC, and lyricist of the time, is said to have written the lyrics to "Rapper's Delight." Big Bank Hank of the Sugarhill Gang had asked Caz for lyrics before the audition for Sylvia Robinson. Caz was never credited.

Also, at the time of the song's release, many New York artists considered "Rapper's Delight" inauthentic and out of touch with the inner-city origins of the hip-hop movement. There were several factors that contributed to this feeling. First, the Sugarhill Gang hadn't struggled on the Bronx hip-hop scene for years as many other artists of the time had. Instead, the group was associated with New Jersey. Second, none of the group members performed as DJs or MCs, both of which were valued roles in hip-hop culture. Finally, the song didn't emphasize the social protest behind hip-hop's development. Rather than

The Sugarhill Gang's "Rapper's Delight" met criticism for being upbeat instead of commenting on the tumultuous culture of the time.

voicing inner-city anger, the song came across as a playful dance number.

On the other hand, the song's success may have come precisely because it was playful rather than political. Wonder Mike explained that the content wasn't very heavy, which made the hip-hop style seem more approachable to new audiences. Even though political messages have been a consistent cornerstone of hip-hop, some argue it would have been hard to introduce both the new style and the powerful political messages at the same time. The Sugarhill Gang took on the new style part, presenting a way to capture the long and interactive form of live hip-hop on a recorded album. That effort cleared the path for other artists to introduce the political part.

> "'Rapper's Delight' is still considered the popular point of departure for contemporary rap music."[1]
>
> —James Braxton Peterson, professor of Africana studies, English, and hip-hop culture

A Trailblazing Female Trio

Following "Rapper's Delight," Sylvia Robinson recruited other groups to her record label. Many of these groups, such as West Street Mob, Funky 4+1, and Crash Crew, shared the Sugarhill Gang's funk and disco sounds. At

Angie B., seen here performing in 2014, went on to become the most successful songwriter and singer of the Sequence.

the same time, the label promoted groups who spread important social messages in their lyrics, including Grandmaster Flash and the Furious Five. Sugar Hill Records also pushed the boundaries of hip-hop by assembling the first all-female recording hip-hop group: the Sequence.

Hailing from Columbia, South Carolina, the three women of the Sequence were Cheryl the Pearl (Cheryl Cook), Blondie (Gwendolyn Chisolm), and Angie B. (Angie Brown Stone). The trio met Robinson when she was on a tour stop with the Sugarhill Gang in Columbia. The young women approached Robinson backstage and asked if they could perform some of their work for her. Impressed, Robinson signed them to her label, and they soon released their first single, "Funk You Up!" From there, the group had a run of singles that made the charts.

Similar to "Rapper's Delight," many of the Sequence's songs played to the popular funk and disco trends of the time. However, in the late 1970s and early 1980s, the Sequence had more chart success than its male counterpart, the Sugarhill Gang. Furthermore, the Sequence also began edging the content of mainstream rap beyond the lighthearted party songs of funk- and disco-styled hip-hop. The group's "love rap" focused on relationships and emotions. Members of the group also stood out as gifted songwriters. In addition to composing their own songs, they wrote lyrics for other Sugar Hill groups, including the Sugarhill Gang.

MULTICULTURAL INFLUENCES

While early hip-hop groups drew on funk and disco to mainstream their work, other influences also helped shape the music. Important among these were Latin and Caribbean influences. Individual artists such as Jamaican-born DJ Kool Herc and Puerto Rican Ken Swift pioneered hip-hop staples of DJ mixing and break dancing, respectively, in part by borrowing from their cultural backgrounds. Meanwhile, in 1981, Mean Machine, a group of Puerto Rican rappers, released their single "Disco Dream" through Sugar Hill Records. The song had a disco funk sound similar to the music of the Sugarhill Gang and the Sequence, but "Disco Dream" also contained rhymes in Spanish.

As the first all-female group to sign with a record label, and as an early group from the South, the Sequence showed hip-hop could open itself to a wide range of artists. Despite the Sequence's success and influence, the group hasn't received as much historical praise or attention as the Sugarhill Gang for its efforts in putting hip-hop on the cultural map. In the case of the Sequence, both the group and the producer, Sylvia Robinson, demonstrate how women had influential roles in the artistic and business sides in the beginnings of hip-hop, even if the scene was largely male dominated.

Run-D.M.C.'s signature style and sound made the group authentic.

Hardcore Replaces Disco Funk

Following Sugar Hill Records'
work to expand the popular
reach of both male and female
hip-hop groups, other early
groups began achieving notable
milestones. An important group
among these was Run-D.M.C.,
which formed in Queens,
New York City, in 1981. The
three members, Run (Joseph
Simmons), D.M.C. (Darryl
McDaniels), and Jam Master Jay
(Jason Mizell) helped transform
hip-hop from its funk and disco
sounds of the late 1970s and
early 1980s to the distinctive,
hardcore East Coast style that
would dominate the rest of the
1980s. The unique sound was
evident in their early hits, such
as "It's Like That" (1983) and
"Hard Times" (1984). These songs

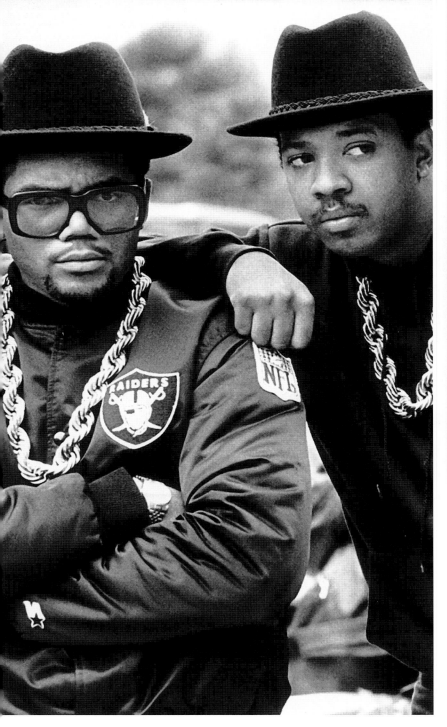

Run-D.M.C.'s efforts to promote a street sound, language, and look helped create a tradition for hip-hop that listeners could identify with.

featured the boom of drum machines, socially conscious lyrics, powerful shouting, and echo rhymes.

Throughout the 1980s, Run-D.M.C. continued developing hip-hop's unique hardcore sound through increasingly complex techniques, including harsh shrieks, scratches, glitches, and hard rock–inspired guitar riffs. Along with these evolving techniques, Run-D.M.C. expanded the social commentary in hip-hop's lyrics, following in the growing tradition of Grandmaster Flash and the Furious Five's "The Message." Run-D.M.C.'s lyrics emphasized the struggles of economic hardship, and the words of the group's songs mirrored the language of the streets, addressing issues listeners cared about in the same terminology they used.

Run-D.M.C.'s Style

Not only did Run-D.M.C. share vocabulary with its audiences, but its members also looked like them. Run-D.M.C. transformed the hip-hop appearance from the flashy, party-ready, disco-inspired getups of the late 1970s to tracksuits, sneakers, and Cazal-brand glasses. Their visual appearance gave the group street authenticity and made political statements as well. For example, Run-D.M.C.'s signature look featured Adidas sneakers without laces, a look that was partly inspired by solidarity with incarcerated minority youth. In prison, shoelaces aren't permitted because they can be used as tools for suicide or violence. Run-D.M.C.'s style gave the message that hip-hop was more than a music genre. It was a culture.

Early groups demonstrated hip-hop music and culture had diverse possibilities. To enter the national scene, though, hip-hop artists first had to tailor the format of their art from long, live performances to short, recorded albums. Second, they had to connect with the music trends popular in the 1970s. Once hip-hop records began spreading to mainstream audiences, artists could start branching out. In the years that followed, groups continued growing in diversity and range.

GOING COMMERCIAL

Run-D.M.C. was so committed to its look members even released a song entitled "My Adidas." The song attracted commercial attention to the group, landing it a contract with Adidas for $1.6 million.[2] The endorsement deal was the first ever between a music act and an athletic company. This deal was just one of many notable firsts that showcased Run-D.M.C.'s combined commercial and critical success. It was the first hip-hop group to be certified gold and platinum, the first hip-hop group to have music on MTV, and the first hip-hop group to appear on the cover of Rolling Stone magazine.

3 DIVERSIFYING HIP-HOP

Groups in the late 1970s and early 1980s showed the ways in which hip-hop could adapt from a live art form to a recording art that could reach listeners on a wide scale. Pioneering hip-hop groups, such as the Sugarhill Gang and the Sequence, carried over popular trends from disco and funk to give hip-hop a familiar sound that appealed to popular audiences. However, once those groups opened the door for other hip-hop artists, hip-hop music began showing off its unique styles. Once hip-hop proved it could be a recording success, groups began incorporating more diversity and pushing the art form in new directions.

The Beastie Boys emerged as the first widespread, successful all-white hip-hop group.

The Beastie Boys perform their high-energy, rebellious hip-hop in 1987.

Hip-Hop's White Rappers

Artists, listeners, and critics often consider hip-hop a black cultural expression rooted in the musical traditions and oral storytelling of the black experience. The championed pioneers of hip-hop were black artists. Furthermore, as socially conscious messages developed into hip-hop hallmarks, lyrics often contrasted black struggle with white privilege to emphasize their messages. White artists

and groups, such as pop band Blondie with its white female singer, attained some success in the early years of hip-hop, but at the same time, white hip-hop artists faced criticisms. These artists had to present themselves as genuine and authentic. The first white group to achieve that authentic feel successfully, gain acceptance, and make a lasting impression on the hip-hop scene was the Beastie Boys.

ORAL STORYTELLING

Within the African-American community, oral storytelling has a long history as a form of art, entertainment, and resistance. Many historians have traced the similarities between stories told by slaves and hip-hop songs. Those stories gave slaves a way to communicate in metaphor, rhyme, and figurative language that their masters didn't understand. Contemporary hip-hop artists continue to use language creatively and according to their own rules to convey political messages.

Beastie Boys

The Beastie Boys originated as a punk rock band under a different name: The Young Aborigines. The group was composed of members Michael Diamond (Mike D), John Berry, Adam Yauch (MCA), and Kate Schellenbach. Schellenbach and Berry left the group after a few years, and Adam Horovitz (Ad-Rock) joined Mike D and MCA. The trio, rebranded as the Beastie Boys, began embracing hip-hop after the release of their 1983 song "Cooky Puss" (sometimes spelled "Cookie Puss"). The song incorporated several hip-hop elements, including sampling, scratching, and rap. Because "Cooky Puss" received such a positive response, the Beastie Boys started experimenting more with the hip-hop form, releasing their debut album, *Licensed to Ill*, with Def Jam and Columbia Records in 1986.

On the album, the Beastie Boys fuse styles, mixing heavy-metal guitar with hip-hop staples, such as beatboxing and assertive vocals. The album also has samples from a wide range of artists, including Led Zeppelin and James Brown. The Beastie Boys' lyrics avoided the socially conscious topics of inner-city message rap because the group members didn't have firsthand experience with those issues. Instead, they used edgy humor and shock value to focus on subjects of adolescent rebellion, such as partying, drugs, and sex. These lyrics, combined with the quirky musical features, made *Licensed to Ill* a unique form of hip-hop that was able to find a place in a predominantly black-oriented art form.

All about the Authenticity

Many black artists accepted the Beastie Boys' work in hip-hop, largely because the group members found a way to be themselves. By this time, hip-hop had grown

WHITE-COLLAR BEASTIE BOYS

The Beastie Boys were all raised in upper-middle-class, white, Jewish families. Mike D's parents were art dealers. MCA's father was an architect, and his mother was a school administrator. Ad-Rock's mother was a painter, and his father an acclaimed playwright. The comfortable backgrounds they experienced contrasted with the financially difficult environments many other hip-hop artists knew so well. Nevertheless, the Beastie Boys were able to communicate their experiences in an authentic way, which contributed to their success.

into an art that valued authenticity. Hip-hop expected artists to express their legitimate views, life experiences, and the issues that affected them in personal ways. The Beastie Boys did that. They didn't front, or pretend to be anything they weren't, to fit into the dominant black culture of hip-hop. By creating unique sounds and lyrics to represent themselves, the Beastie Boys showed hip-hop's flexibility to reach across race and genre lines. Throughout its decades-long career, the group collaborated with all kinds of musicians. It drew inspiration from diverse sources as well, even incorporating songs from groups such as legendary British pop band the Beatles into its music. In showing this variety, it set a precedent for artists and

The Beastie Boys often collaborated with Run-D.M.C., further cementing their place in the hip-hop realm.

listeners from different racial backgrounds to engage in the world of hip-hop.

Female Artists Draw Attention

The group Salt-N-Pepa brought more change to hip-hop, broadening its gender appeal. Although Salt-N-Pepa wasn't the first all-female hip-hop group, it was the first female group to receive several significant

nominations and awards, including a Grammy. Moreover, Salt-N-Pepa took the Sequence's early feminine rap about love and emotion and pushed it further to create a unique style of hip-hop. This style embraced a strong female identity that stood up to male-dominated hip-hop, which tended to objectify women. Instead of reinforcing aggressive, abusive, sexualized stereotypes of women, Salt-N-Pepa showed ways women could spread empowering images through their music.

Salt-N-Pepa's Statements on Style and Gender

Originally from Queens, the group of three—Salt (Cheryl James), Pepa (Sandra Denton), and Spinderella (Deidra Roper) released its first album, *Hot, Cool & Vicious*, in 1986. On this record, and on the four others that followed, Salt-N-Pepa's songs contain forceful messages about gender. They give women power in choosing relationships and offer warnings against men who would take advantage of them. For example, in the song "Tramp" (1986), Salt-N-Pepa use a confident rapping style to tell women they don't have to be "victim[s] of circumstance" and they can stand up to men who are "stupid and rude." They encourage women to shout "Don't touch my body!" to those men who only care about a woman's physical appearance. Salt-N-Pepa matched these

SPINDERELLA

Spinderella took on the role of DJ in the group Salt-N-Pepa. For most of Salt-N-Pepa's albums, Deidra (Dee Dee) Roper served as Spinderella, but she wasn't the original. When she was 16 years old, Roper replaced Latoya Hanson after a few other auditions and changes to the group's DJ position. On the group's second album, *A Salt with a Deadly Pepa* (1988), there is a song about Spinderella, "Spinderella's Not a Fella (But a Girl DJ)." The song addresses the misconception that all good DJs are men.

Salt-N-Pepa feminized hip-hop clothing and jewelry, pairing oversized jackets and chains with short shorts, leggings, and tight tops.

lyrics with a distinctive look that reaffirmed female power. They wore a mix of hip-hop clothing and distinctively black hairstyles, such as short, asymmetrical cuts, to reinforce their identity as both strongly feminine and strongly black.

One of the reasons Salt-N-Pepa was so successful is because it advanced serious gender messages while also exploring the playful, cheeky, and partying aspects of hip-hop. By exploring different sides of the music, Salt-N-Pepa laid a path for women in the industry to overturn the male-dominated culture of hip-hop and some of the sexist claims it spread.

> "It's very comical, it's very fun. It flipped the script in terms of talking about men in the same way they talk about women."[1]
>
> —Salt, commenting on the group's 1993 song "Shoop"

Breaking Out

If the late 1970s and early 1980s were about establishing the roots of hip-hop in form and popularity, the later 1980s and early 1990s were all about branching out. These years saw hip-hop diversify across race and gender as new groups built on the work of those who came before them. The Beastie Boys and Salt-N-Pepa were dominant on the hip-hop scene as the 1990s began, and both groups were regularly nominated for Grammy and MTV Video Music Awards throughout the decade. Salt-N-Pepa finally won a Grammy for Best Rap Performance by a Duo or Group in 1995 (for "None of Your Business"), and an MTV Video Music Award for Best R&B Video in 1994 (for "Whatta Man"). These successes indicated hip-hop was no longer in

Pepa, Spinderella, and Salt react to and accept the award for "Whatta Man" at the 1994 MTV Video Music Awards.

its beginning phases. Hip-hop had become so established in popular music that diverse groups could broaden its reach and steer it in creative new directions.

4 WEST COAST
HIP-HOP

Groups not only grew more diverse in race and gender during the late 1980s and early 1990s, but they also began expanding geographically. In its early years, hip-hop culture centered on the East Coast, particularly in New York. California groups, such as N.W.A (Niggaz With Attitude), Cypress Hill, and Tha Dogg Pound, gained momentum as the 1990s pressed on, shifting the map of hip-hop in the United States. As West Coast groups stepped into the limelight, hip-hop experienced new waves of innovation. But some of this creativity was undermined by new controversies and criticisms. Of particular concern was the West Coast gangsta style, which led many within

Dr. Dre speaks at N.W.A's induction to the Rock & Roll Hall of Fame in 2016.

and outside of the music industry to believe hip-hop had taken a dangerous turn.

West Coast Gangsta Style

In 1988, the six members of N.W.A—MC Ren (Lorenzo Patterson), Eazy-E (Eric Wright), Ice Cube (O'Shea Jackson), Dr. Dre (Andre Young), DJ Yella (Antoine Carraby), and Arabian Prince (Kim Nazel)—released their first album, *Straight Outta Compton*. Named after the group's hometown in California, the record was a confrontational gangsta rap piece with a hardcore sound and seething lyrics about racism, injustices, and corrupt national authority. N.W.A wasn't the first group to address these topics. Some East Coast groups also spread an anti-authority message, as Public Enemy did in its hit "Fight the Power" (1989). However, N.W.A's aggressive attack on authority throughout its first album cemented that

GANGSTA LIFE

In the late 1980s and early 1990s, the music industry began using the term *gangsta* to describe gangster rap. The spelling comes from African-American vernacular, which changes the *-er* of *gangster* to an *a*. This subgenre is distinguished from other types of hip-hop, such as message rap, through its direct involvement in gang violence, drug use, crime, and misogyny. Gangsta artists often present themselves as having lived that lifestyle, and they use music as a way to assert power and strength.

N.W.A's *Straight Outta Compton* song lyrics illustrate the group's violent, gangsta style.

subject matter as a cornerstone of the new West Coast gangsta style.

N.W.A's West Coast gangsta rap had a sharper edge than the message rap of the East Coast. That edge was a reflection of the circumstances in Compton and other areas of Los Angeles, California, during the 1980s and early 1990s. At the time, the city was a hotbed of gang violence

HIP-HOP ON THE BIG SCREEN

Though N.W.A broke up in the early 1990s, interest renewed in the group with the 2015 movie *Straight Outta Compton*. Based on the true story of the group and its work, the movie focuses especially on Eazy-E's journey from drug dealer to influential rapper and producer to an untimely death from AIDS complications in 1995. *Straight Outta Compton* was a success with moviegoers and critics. Furthermore, it joins in the tradition of using film to advance understanding of hip-hop's artistry, history, and culture. Movies have been an effective tool for spreading that understanding since the 1980s. Films such as *Wild Style*, *Breakin'*, *Breakin' 2*, and *Beat Street* helped popularize hip-hop nationally and carry the music to new, international markets.

and drug activity, which often resulted in clashes between inner-city youth and police. Adding to the unrest, government officials imposed divisive measures such as curfews and frequent police stops. These stops affected minority youth more than other groups of people, and young men were often forced to lie on the ground or against police cars while officials checked their names for gang membership. The feeling of constant oppression, combined with other problems, such as persistent poverty, contributed to the anger expressed in N.W.A's music.

Many of the songs on *Straight Outta Compton* and N.W.A's second album, *Niggaz4Life* (1991), contain explicit wording as well as crime-ridden and sexist depictions of gangsta life. These depictions stoked both the group's controversy as well as its popularity. *Straight Outta Compton* has sold more than three million copies, going triple platinum, including prolific sales with white suburban listeners.[1] Audiences may have taken an interest in N.W.A's music because they shared outrage over the deep oppression minority youth felt. On the other hand, researchers also note white and middle-class listeners would have had little experience with the kinds of oppression N.W.A rapped about. Instead, those listeners

All the members of N.W.A were from Compton, a city in the Los Angeles area.

represented a cultural taste for violence. Whatever the reason, N.W.A drew a wide and diverse audience, and it set the stage for the West Coast's prominence in hip-hop.

Cypress Hill

The diverse spread of West Coast hip-hop continued with Cypress Hill, a multiethnic group that went platinum with its first album and multiplatinum with music that followed. The members of Cypress Hill came together in South Gate, California, in the late 1980s. The original group was made up of five artists from different backgrounds. There were two Cuban brothers, Sen Dog (Senen Reyes) and Mellow Man Ace (Sergio Reyes). DJ Muggs (Lawrence

Members B-Real and Sen Dog bring different cultural backgrounds to Cypress Hill.

Muggerud) was an Italian American who grew up in Queens but moved to Los Angeles as a teenager. B-Real's (Louis Freese) family was of Mexican and Cuban heritage. Ace quickly left the group to pursue a solo career, but the remaining members released their first album in 1991, also named *Cypress Hill*. The album debuted with strong reviews, and it had several charting singles, including "Latin Lingo" and "How I Could Just Kill a Man."

Cypress Hill's music tied into the growing West Coast hip-hop culture in many ways. The group advocated illegal behaviors, especially drug use, and it indulged in violent lyrics to vent frustrations against the treatment of minority youth by police and government policies. The 1991 song "Pigs," for example, is all about graphic revenge on corrupt police officers. However, this kind of hardcore gangsta content didn't dominate all of Cypress Hill's songs. The group showed a range of musical styles, from punk to reggae to rock, with mellow beats, humor, and a distinctive high-pitched, nasal sound from B-Real.

Cypress Hill also quickly realized it could use its musical, racial, and ethnic diversity to the group's advantage. In songs such as

> "We feel the. . . Mexicans, the Chinese, white kids, it don't matter."[2]
>
> —DJ Muggs

"Latin Lingo," the group mixes standard English, hip-hop slang, and Spanish, calling the blend "Spanglish" and "funky bilingo." The language mixing was a unique way for Cypress Hill to reinforce hip-hop's anti-authority messages and draw young audiences in. By breaking the rules of standard English and creating a new hybrid language, the group drew young listeners from different backgrounds, all of whom could find their experiences in the music.

Gangsta Rap Pushes the Limits

Alongside the evolving sounds and increasing diversity of West Coast hip-hop, there also came growing controversies. N.W.A's music was purposefully angry and extreme to express the real

"PIGS"

The song "Pigs" had special meaning to B-Real. He wrote the song in a fury after being harassed by police one night. In his explanation of the song, B-Real notes he was using the phone outside a fast-food restaurant when police approached and ordered him to put his hands on his car. At the time, B-Real had no weapons or drugs, and he hadn't done anything to cause a problem. B-Real believes the sole reason for the confrontation had to do with race and identity. "We looked like thugs, so they basically treated us like thugs," B-Real recalls.[3] When the police supervisor arrived and heard what had happened, he told his officers to apologize. However, the apology didn't make up for the experience. The harsh words in "Pigs" express the anger B-Real felt based on that encounter and others like it.

frustrations black men felt. Cypress Hill incorporated some of that same fury, and even its mellower songs celebrated illegal behavior. West Coast artists defended their music and its subject matter as forms of rebellion against racist, classist power structures in the United States. However, opponents argued artists incorporated illicit topics into their music too freely, presenting dangerous behavior as entertainment. This point of view resulted in concerns about the direction of gangsta hip-hop. Tha Dogg Pound is one group that received this kind of criticism because it readily used profanity and referenced misogyny, violence, and sex in its songs.

Tha Dogg Pound, a duo formed between Kurupt (Ricardo Emmanuel Brown) and Daz Dillinger (Delmar Drew Arnaud), started in Long Beach, California, in 1992. After working as artists on Dr. Dre's first solo album, *The Chronic* (1992), the two paired up to form Tha Dogg Pound at Dr. Dre's suggestion. Tha Dogg Pound went on to perform in parts of Snoop Dogg's debut, *Doggystyle*, as well as on some soundtracks for the label Death Row Records. Daz and Snoop Dogg are cousins. In 1995, Tha Dogg Pound released its own album, *Dogg Food*, also with Death Row Records. The album shot to the top of the *Billboard* charts, receiving praise for advancing the sound

Daz Dillinger, *left*, and Kurupt, *right*, perform in California in 2013.

of West Coast hip-hop, maintaining a high production value, and featuring other artists. Nevertheless, the album found itself at the center of much debate as some people grew wary of the gangsta lifestyle. Time

Warner, for example, cut its business ties with Death Row Records over the album. Tha Dogg Pound and its supporters saw that move as an attack on their art, life experiences, and right to free speech. On the other hand, opponents viewed it as a necessary step to discourage a dangerous lifestyle.

> "Ours is a street thing—that's our voice, and it's hard. . . . But it's not necessarily a negative message. It's hard being a man on the street, too, being yourself. We deal with that."[4]
>
> —Daz

The controversy grew as Tha Dogg Pound became involved in high-profile feuds with other hip-hop artists. The music video for one track on *Dogg Food*, "New York, New York," showed the group, along with special featured artist Snoop Dogg, towering over the city in larger-than-life size. They stomped through the streets, kicked over buildings, and wreaked havoc in a boastful way. According to Kurupt, the song wasn't originally supposed to be a diss track. In fact, it was supposed to be a tribute to hip-hop's New York roots. However, the song morphed into a diss track after East Coast artists misinterpreted the video as disrespectful. On another track, "Dogg Pound Gangstaz," Tha Dogg Pound openly dissed Cleveland-formed group Bone Thugs-N-Harmony because of bad blood between their record labels. Though these feuds eventually resolved, at the time, outsiders saw them as confirmation of gangsta hip-hop's aggressive behavior. The conflicts seemed to present hip-hop artists as people with hot tempers and fierce egos who could be provoked easily into word wars and acts of violence.

With the success of West Coast gangsta hip-hop throughout the late 1980s and early 1990s, groups such as N.W.A, Cypress Hill, and Tha Dogg Pound proved hip-hop popularity wasn't limited to one small pocket of the country. West Coast groups also helped increase racial diversity in the industry, and they gave a loud voice to the justifiable anger of many minority men. On the other hand, gangsta rap's messages embraced dangerous behaviors—drug use, abuse of women, revenge, and violence. Disagreements stirred up on the West Coast over the direction of hip-hop would continue into the following years as East Coast artists worked to reenergize their music.

EAST COAST VS. WEST COAST

The problems resulting from "New York, New York" involved Tha Dogg Pound directly in the much-discussed East Coast/ West Coast feud. Hip-hop scholar Mark Anthony Neal explains that the conflict arose as the popularity of West Coast artists began to challenge the East Coast as the longstanding center of hip-hop. At the heart of this feud "was a fundamental belief that the experiences of those on one coast marked them as more authentic—more gangsta, more ghetto, more hardcore—than those on the other."[5] Verbal and physical attacks came from both coasts, culminating in the shooting deaths of West Coast rapper Tupac Shakur and East Coast rapper the Notorious B.I.G. (Christopher Wallace).

5 EAST COAST GROUPS

As West Coast gangsta hip-hop took off in the 1990s, East Coast groups innovated their styles in what has come to be known as the East Coast Renaissance. During this time, groups such as A Tribe Called Quest focused on innovative, collective avenues instead of gangsta rap. On the other hand, groups such as Mobb Deep incorporated signatures of hip-hop's dark and dangerous edge, and the Wu-Tang Clan presented hip-hop as music filled with struggle. This period marked a time when hip-hop was challenged by negative uses of the art form. However, New York artists responded to these challenges with creative expressions that exposed both the unity and the discord hip-hop could convey.

East Coast group A Tribe Called Quest veered away from the bicoastal
jvelry and gangsta rap controversies in the 1990s.

Creating a Collective

While still high school students in Queens, Q-Tip (born Jonathan Davis, later Kamaal Ibn John Fareed), Phife Dawg (Malik Isaac Taylor), Ali Shaheed Muhammad, and Jarobi White joined together to form A Tribe Called Quest. They released their first album, *People's Instinctive Travels and the Paths of Rhythm*, in 1990, and then four more albums in the following eight years. A Tribe Called Quest's early music didn't receive much mainstream attention, but it garnered praise from music critics as well as listeners seeking an alternative to the materialistic, misogynistic, and violence-riddled hip-hop popular with West Coast gangsta groups. Instead of the harsh rhymes of West Coast gangsta hip-hop, A Tribe Called Quest's songs sampled jazz, incorporated lyrical melodies from many different instruments and natural sounds, and

ZULU NATION

A Tribe Called Quest promoted Afrocentrism, as did DJ Afrika Bambaataa. He led the Zulu Nation movement in the 1970s to transform his former gang, the Black Spades, into a peaceful cultural and artistic center for hip-hop. Zulu Nation combined 1960s principles of black pride and peaceful revolution to present young blacks with an alternative to the dangers of street life and gang violence. Zulu Nation encouraged youth to explore their racial identities, connect with their communities, and channel their energy in positive, creative expressions instead of negative behavior.

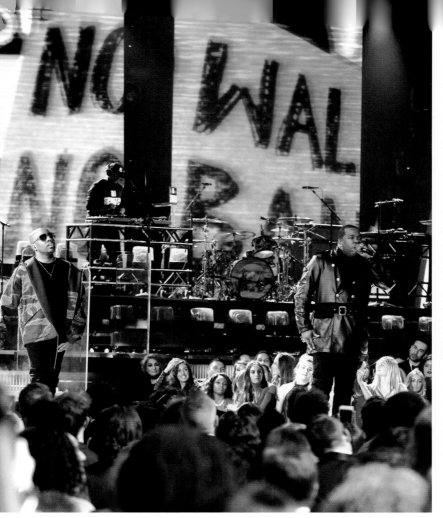

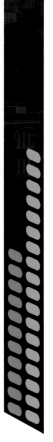

A Tribe Called Quest gave a very politically fueled performance at the 2017 Grammys.

embraced a quieter, more poetic attitude. Its songs still had important socially conscious lyrics, but as an interviewer would later note, "the vibe was different— loose, fun, with head-nodding beats pulled from sources far and wide."[1]

Because A Tribe Called Quest was known for its collaborations and sampling, it's no surprise the group became part of a collective: the Native Tongues posse. Other artists in the collective included De La Soul, the Jungle Brothers, and Queen Latifah, among others. Together, these artists focused on presenting a positive, Afrocentric music culture. Afrocentrism encouraged young black hip-hop listeners to think of Africa as an inspirational homeland, to take pride in their ancestral history, and to feel a connection to people of color around the world. A Tribe Called Quest highlighted its outlook in songs, including "Can I Kick It" and "Push It Along." These songs described what it meant to be tribal and to adopt Afrocentric living.

Energizing the East Coast

A Tribe Called Quest wasn't the only East Coast group working to promote a united spirit in minority communities. The Wu-Tang Clan aimed for a similar goal. Under the leadership of RZA (Robert Diggs), the group of nine formed in 1992 and released its first album, *Enter the Wu-Tang (36 Chambers)*,

> " And that's what Wu-Tang was: It was a home-cooked meal of hip-hop. Of the real people." [2]
>
> —RZA

the following year. Other members included Raekwon the Chef (Corey Woods), Ol' Dirty Bastard (Russell Jones), Ghostface Killah (Dennis Coles), Masta Killa (Jamel Irief, born Elgin Turner), Inspectah Deck (Jason Hunter), Method Man (Clifford Smith), Genius/GZA (Gary Grice), and U-God (Lamont Hawkins). Forming within a few years of one another, the Wu-Tang Clan and A Tribe Called Quest had much in common in their attitudes. Because the Wu-Tang Clan is such a large group, it also represented a collective African-American spirit and community, and it was interested in the strength of that community. However, the group saw building that strength as part of a wide-scale struggle, which gave its music a darker edge than that of A Tribe Called Quest.

The feeling of struggle is clear even in the group's name. *Wu-Tang* refers to the kung fu movies and martial arts mind-set that influenced the group. Amy Chasteen

MARTIAL ARTS INSPIRATION

The Wu-Tang Clan's leader, RZA, has been particularly outspoken about his interest in martial arts. He recalls practicing martial arts on Staten Island when he was only 11. Later in life, he trained and was ordained as a disciple of Shaolin for his work. Shaolin is one of the oldest kung fu styles in the world. RZA has also written and produced music for martial arts films, including *Kill Bill* and *Ghost Dog: The Way of the Samurai*.

The multitude of different voices gives Wu-Tang Clan's music its gritty, relatable, versatile, and down-to-earth feel.

and Thomas Shriver, professors who study hip-hop, explain that for the group, "rapping is a form of battle, much like Kung-Fu, that requires knowledge, a mastery of techniques, and a willingness to strive for personal and

social strength and success."[3] The Wu-Tang Clan's battle was against the many negative circumstances minority groups faced in the inner city, and it was rooted in a desire to change that reality.

Unlike the middle-class members of A Tribe Called Quest, Wu-Tang's members had grown up in and around the housing projects of Brooklyn and Staten Island, where they saw neglected living conditions, violence of all kinds, drug activity, lack of opportunity, and many homeless people. They openly acknowledged they were dropouts, felons, and street kids. These topics appeared often in their music because they wanted to shed light on the problems and present the real issues people dealt with every day on the street.

A NEW BUSINESS MODEL

The Wu-Tang Clan had a unique structure and business model that allowed it to reach throughout the hip-hop industry. In their contracts, which were unique for the time, members of the group had the freedom to put out solo albums with any record label they wanted. Meanwhile, members also remained loyal to the larger group, releasing collective albums and frequently guest appearing on each other's solo projects. As a result, the nine members acted more like a dynamic supergroup than one unchanging unit. This supergroup model grew more popular among hip-hop artists in the 2000s.

To draw attention to those issues, the Wu-Tang Clan focused on reaching wide audiences with a diverse array of styles and sounds. "Protect Ya Neck," the first song on the group's first album, serves as a good example of its approach. On the track, each member of the Wu-Tang Clan takes on one verse to introduce himself and his style to the listeners, which was important to the group's message and identity. While other hip-hop tracks frequently incorporated multiple voices into individual songs, no other group had included as many as the Wu-Tang Clan.

> "[Their music was] rugged raps about the urban underworld . . . skeletal beats laced with haunting strings, piano, and snippets of soulful vocals."[4]
>
> — Rolling Stone *magazine on Mobb Deep*

Hardcore Hits New York

Other East Coast Renaissance groups also addressed life's hardships through their hip-hop, but some, such as Mobb Deep, took on an even bleaker point of view. Havoc (Kejuan Muchita) and Prodigy (Albert Johnson) formed Mobb Deep in New York in 1990. In 1993, while still teenagers, they released their first album, *Juvenile Hell*. That album didn't receive good reviews, nor did it sell well. However, their next two albums, *The Infamous* (1995) and *Hell on Earth* (1996), put them on the scene as innovators in East Coast hip-hop. Their use of piano loops was one of the most distinctive and original trademarks of their music.

Havoc, *left*, and Prodigy, *right*, formed Mobb Deep, one of the most acclaimed groups of East Coast hardcore hip-hop.

The haunting sound of Mobb Deep's music was meant to echo the pair's backgrounds. The neighborhoods Havoc and Prodigy grew up in (Queensbridge, Queens, and

Hempstead, Long Island) were tough neighborhoods where kids spent most of their time in the projects and on welfare, feeling angry and desperate. Prodigy remembers, "A lot of negativity was going on around us. A lot of crime, a lot of shootings, drug dealings, a lot of craziness." He also explains, "We experienced a lot of deaths around us . . . a lot of our friends got murdered."[5] The strong feelings from these experiences found an outlet in the lyrics and the style of the beats.

> **"**I was an angry kid going through what I was going through, so the first thing that attracted me to hip-hop was it was so aggressive, and it was a way that I could get my anger out.**"**[6]
>
> —Prodigy

Interestingly, A Tribe Called Quest member Q-Tip mentored Mobb Deep, even though the duo veered away from the fun and positivity of the Native Tongues. This collaboration showed hip-hop could at times be uplifting, while at other times it grappled with serious issues. The Wu-Tang Clan demonstrated this idea as well. After so much attention on the violence of gangsta rap and the bitter bicoastal rivalry, the combination of positive and negative in the East Coast Renaissance was a valuable lesson.

6 MIDWEST AND SOUTH GROUPS

Throughout the 1990s, regional identity carried a strong weight with hip-hop artists. The East and West Coasts dominated the industry throughout the 1980s and into the mid-1990s. However, by the late 1990s, innovative hip-hop groups were attracting attention to other regions. Groups from the Midwest and the South began reaching their peaks and gaining national success in the late 1990s and early 2000s. These groups opened hip-hop's borders and ushered in new possibilities for the sounds, people, and issues represented in the industry.

Bone Thugs-N-Harmony

In the Midwest, the members of Bone Thugs-N-Harmony were aggressively searching

for a label to put their Cleveland, Ohio, sound on the map. Members Krayzie Bone (Anthony Henderson), Wish Bone (Charles Scruggs), Layzie Bone (Steven Howse), Bizzy Bone (Bryon Anthony McCane II), and Flesh-N-Bone (Stanley Howse, Layzie's younger brother, who joined a bit later than the others) signed to Ruthless Records in 1993, with former N.W.A member Eazy-E as their mentor. Though Ruthless Records was a Los Angeles–based label, Bone Thugs-N-Harmony often referred to its Midwest roots. For example, at the 1995 Source Awards, Krayzie Bone took center stage in a Cleveland Indians baseball T-shirt as the group performed its hit "Thuggish Ruggish Bone." Through its efforts, Bone Thugs-N-Harmony became an important force

Bone Thugs-N-Harmony was named favorite hip-hop group at the 2007 American Music Awards.

in shifting hip-hop's vision to include the middle of the country in addition to the coasts.

Midwest hip-hop was harder to define than the East Coast and West Coast styles that came before it. Bone Thugs-N-Harmony collaborated with the most well-known artists from both coasts, including the Notorious B.I.G. and Big Pun from the East and Tupac and Eazy-E from the West. At the same time, group members brought their own elements to the music, creating a distinct mix and an original sound. They drew on some of the violent content of gangsta and hardcore hip-hop, but they combined that with fast rhymes, skilled vocal harmonies, and a unique emphasis on spirituality. In "Crossroads," for instance, the lyrics and the music video are full of images about death, the afterlife, and the journeying souls of departed loved ones. Bone Thugs-N-Harmony's original approach to hip-hop proved to be successful. "Crossroads" won a Grammy in 1997. The group also won American Music Awards in 1998 and 2007, and it was the first group from the Midwest to go platinum in sales.

The Dirty South

While Bone Thugs-N-Harmony carved out a place on the map for Midwest groups, others were working to do the same in the South. Similar to Midwest hip-hop, Southern hip-hop was hard to define. Goodie Mob, a group from Atlanta, Georgia, used the term *Dirty South* as one of its song titles on a track from its 1995 album, *Soul Food*, and the term developed into a key expression for the region's hip-hop. The phrase had already been circulating for years on the club scene in Southern cities. However, the song focused on the phrase, with the refrain asking, "What you . . . know about the Dirty South?" The question pointed out how much the hip-hop industry had ignored the South.

SOUTHERN ISOLATION

An attitude of regional superiority was floating around during the 1990s because of the high-profile East and West Coast rivalry. There was a general trend toward defending one's region without letting others in. Media and investors were reluctant to spend money on little-known Southern artists without as much hip-hop history as East and West Coast names. As a result, radio stations and magazines didn't spend their resources promoting Southern artists, which kept them in isolation.

Young black men in Southern cities experienced many of the same hardships as black men in the inner cities of Los Angeles and New York. Southern cities also had the added ghosts of Jim Crow laws and slavery in their pasts.

BEHIND
THE SONG

"CROSSROADS": AN HOMAGE TO FRIENDS AND FAMILY

The version of "Crossroads" released to radio is an homage to Eazy-E, who died of AIDS complications just four months before Bone Thugs-N-Harmony released its first album, *E. 1999 Eternal* (July 1995). Eazy had given the group members their first chance and had been their mentor, so they thought it would be appropriate to redo the song lyrics to include his name. The revised version also mentions Wish Bone's Uncle Charles and other family and friends who had passed away. The original song was composed in honor of the group's deceased friend Wally, but Krayzie Bone explains that many other loved ones died in a short time just before the album's release. The group wanted to dedicate the song to all those people, so they remixed it. "Crossroads" was and remains Bone Thugs-N-Harmony's most popular song because the emotional message touches people at a personal level, often moving fans to tears during live concerts.

Eazy-E, member of
N.W.A and mentor to
Bone Thugs-N-Harmony,
was regarded by
many in the industry
as the Godfather of
Gangsta Rap.

Artists such as the four members of Goodie Mob—CeeLo Green (Thomas DeCarlo Callaway), Khujo (Willie Edward Knighton Jr.), T-Mo (Robert Barnett), and Big Gipp (Cameron Gipp)—who led the way in Southern hip-hop, had experienced exclusion at nearly every level. Therefore, the exclusion from the hip-hop industry as well was especially maddening.

Outkast

This feeling of isolation was developed further by Outkast, a group that worked closely with Goodie Mob. In fact, there were times when the two groups worked together as a united collective, calling themselves the Dungeon Family. The Outkast duo of André 3000 (André Benjamin) and Big Boi (Antwan Patton) was from the mostly black neighborhood of East Point, Georgia, and even its name—"Outkast"—labeled the group as a hip-hop outsider. Its first album, *Southernplayalisticadillacmuzik*, went platinum in 1995 and earned the group a Source Award for Best New Artist. However, when the duo ventured onstage to receive the award, the New York audience booed them.

> "The South got somethin' to say. And that's all I've got to say."[1]
>
> —André 3000, in response to the New York crowd that booed the group

Outkast is known for its fun style and upbeat songs.

Together with Goodie Mob, Outkast showed who the
Dirty South artists were and what they had to say. In music
that was alternatively soulful and hardcore crunk, these
groups rapped about the corrupt attitudes and systems

CRUNK

Crunk is an energetic dance and rapping style associated with Southern hip-hop since the 1990s. The raps include group chants, call-and-response, and fast, choppy beats. The dances feature fast-paced jumping, stomping, and arm-throwing to the beats, along with juking. Juking has been described as stepping, sliding, and toe-tip spinning. The word *crunk* is thought to have come from the slang term "cranked up," which means to get pumped up or energized.

that oppressed young black men in the South: a broken judicial system, white supremacy, struggling single mothers, and black-on-black violence. Despite the lack of acceptance early on, Goodie Mob and Outkast kept producing records that sold well, proving their legitimacy as hip-hop artists. By the early 2000s, Southern artists made up almost 60 percent of the hit singles on the hip-hop charts.[2] Goodie Mob had lost some momentum by this time because of CeeLo's departure from the group, but Outkast had gained momentum, earning six Grammys by 2004.

Female Groups Lead Hip-Hop in the South

The South was also a growing center for female groups. In Atlanta in 1991, the trio of T-Boz (Tionne Watkins), Left Eye (Lisa Lopes), and Chilli (Rozonda Thomas) formed TLC. The

Chilli, T-Boz, and Left Eye won an award for "Waterfalls" at the MTV Video Music Awards in 1995.

next year, LaFace, the same label Goodie Mob and Outkast signed with, released TLC's first album, *Oooooooohhh...On the TLC Tip,* to positive critical and audience reviews. It was the first major success for the LaFace label, and TLC's popularity only deepened with its next albums, *CrazySexyCool* (1994) and *FanMail* (1999). These albums led to several award nominations and four Grammy wins between 1996 and 2000.

TLC's music didn't follow the style or content of Dirty South male groups. Instead, TLC had more in common with its female predecessors the Sequence and Salt-N-Pepa. TLC presented music about strong women who had control of sex and power, and who tore down men who would use and abuse them. Also like those predecessors, TLC produced genre-mixing music to include pop and R&B elements alongside hip-hop elements, such as sampling. As a result, TLC's music had a cross-regional flavor instead of a uniquely local sound. Though its content wasn't "Dirty South" like Goodie Mob's and Outkast's, TLC's widely popular work contributed to the South's authority as the hip-hop epicenter in the new millennium. Moreover, the group's success showed that as the geographic borders of hip-hop were shattered, so too were borders of genre and gender. Those revelations paved the way for other Southern female groups with crossover appeal, including Destiny's Child, the Houston-formed group that launched Beyoncé's career.

LISA LOPES'S TRAGEDY

Lopes died in a head-on collision in 2002 while driving in Honduras. Earlier in life, Lopes had experienced a great deal of tragedy. Her father was an abusive alcoholic. Lopes also drank heavily and found herself in a violent relationship. However, in her late twenties, Lopes began cleaning up her life, even going on retreats to Honduras to find spiritual peace and healing. She was on one of these retreats when her fatal accident occurred.

TLC accepts the Best Group Video award for "No Scrubs" at the MTV Video Music Awards in 1999.

The late 1990s and early 2000s saw major changes in the hip-hop landscape. After years of attention focused on the East Coast, West Coast, and rivalry between the two, groups from the Midwest and the South worked hard to chisel out a place on the stage and offer a fresh perspective on hip-hop culture. These groups varied widely even in their own regions. Collectively, though, they showed hip-hop was a flexible art form that could stretch to represent a variety of people speaking from a range of places and life experiences.

7 SUPERGROUPS
OF HIP-HOP

While the diverse geographic spread of hip-hop continued into the late 2000s and beyond, another trend emerged: supergroups. In hip-hop and other musical fields, supergroups are composed of artists who join forces after they've already established themselves as solo performers. Hip-hop supergroups weren't a new concept in the 2000s. Nas, Foxy Brown, Snoop Dogg, Eminem, CeeLo, André 3000, and many others found themselves working in supergroups on occasion. Though not new, hip-hop supergroups had a noticeable presence in the later years of the 2000s and into the 2010s. Some of these supergroups have enjoyed long-term success, while others failed to meet high expectations. Regardless of success or

Supergroup Child Rebel Soldier members Kanye West, *right*, and Pharrell Williams, *left*, have gone on to have very successful careers.

83

THE CRS BRAND

When Lupe, Kanye, and Pharrell first came together, they had bold ideas for the direction of the CRS brand. They considered plans not just for music but for art and fashion-based projects as well. They also considered involving other hip-hop artists. For instance, they thought about having Common come aboard with some clothing designs. The original concept was to make the brand as wide-reaching and outlandish as possible because of the extraordinary talent of the artists involved.

failure, these supergroups emphasize how far hip-hop has come in generating popular artists with multiple options for long-term music production.

The High-Powered Supergroup

In 2007, Kanye West, Lupe Fiasco, and Pharrell Williams teamed up to form the supergroup Child Rebel Soldier (CRS). At the time of CRS's formation, Kanye West had already released three solo albums: *The College Dropout* (2004), *Late Registration* (2005), and *Graduation* (2007). With these albums, Kanye was making a name for himself as an innovative and outspoken industry leader. Meanwhile, Lupe Fiasco (Wasalu Muhammad Jaco) and Pharrell Williams were making their own marks on the music scene. By 2007, Lupe had completed two of his own well-acclaimed, chart-topping albums, *Lupe Fiasco's Food & Liquor* (2006) and *Lupe Fiasco's The Cool* (2007), and Pharrell had put out his Grammy-nominated debut solo album, *In My Mind* (2006).

CRS made its musical debut with "Us Placers," a song from Kanye's mixtape *Can't Tell Me Nothing* (2007), which released just before *Graduation*. There was immediate excitement from listeners, industry professionals, and the artists themselves over the group's potential. Throughout the next year, the trio seemed on track to produce larger projects, perhaps even an album. In 2008, CRS released the song "Everyone Nose," a remix of a track by N.E.R.D., another group Pharrell was involved in. That same year, the three participated in Kanye's very successful Glow in the Dark Tour, which also featured Rihanna and N.E.R.D.

However, CRS's music stalled after that, and it didn't release another song until 2011, when "Don't Stop!" was played on a free giveaway series organized by Kanye. Plans for an album, which the group had entitled *God Unwilling*, eventually fell through, and Lupe announced on social media that CRS had ended. CRS never gave an explanation for the breakup, but earlier

> "I always tell my fans: Do you ask Kanye [about the CRS album] as much as you ask me this? Or do you ask Pharrell this? It seems like I'm the spokesperson for Child Rebel Soldier somehow."[1]
>
> —*Lupe Fiasco*

interviews indicated members of the group were too busy to collaborate on a full album. There were also hints that personality differences and expectations may have played a part. The breakup pointed to some of the problems that can arise when well-established artistic professionals work together. These problems include time, differences of opinion, personality clashes, creative disagreements, and business and financial complications.

WATCH THE THRONE

Kanye West's collaboration with Jay Z was one of the major projects slowing CRS's album progress. Kanye and Jay Z's album, *Watch the Throne*, came out in 2011. In addition to combining the skills of the two very influential headliners, the album also draws on the talent of other hip-hop leaders, including Beyoncé, Frank Ocean, Q-Tip, and RZA. There was speculation that the album might lead to a supergroup duo between the artists, but *Watch the Throne* has been the only record-length collaboration between the two.

Long-Lasting Supergroups

Other supergroups have had more success at seeing long-term projects through. Slaughterhouse has been one of the best examples of a supergroup achieving success on major projects over a span of several years. The supergroup released its self-titled first album in 2009 with members Joe Budden, Joell Ortiz, Crooked I (born Dominick Wickliffe and also known as KXNG Crooked), and Royce Da 5'9" (Ryan Daniel Montgomery). The artists banded together after Ortiz, Crooked I, and Royce appeared as guest performers in the song "Slaughterhouse," a track from Budden's album *Halfway House* (2008).

Though all members came to the supergroup with some industry experience, each artist had a unique background. Crooked I came from the West Coast (Long Beach), Royce from the Midwest (Detroit, Michigan), and Ortiz and Budden from the East Coast (Brooklyn and

Slaughterhouse's members allowed their varied backgrounds and differences to enhance their music rather than cause problems.

Harlem, respectively). One of the keys to the group's success has been its ability to fuse those backgrounds. Reviews have praised Slaughterhouse's use of these wide geographic influences. Slaughterhouse members also understand the value of diversity and its role in the creative process. Instead of seeing the supergroup collaboration as a limitation or as a distraction from other creative projects, they see it as a way to push themselves and their art even further. As of 2016, Slaughterhouse had released five albums and mixtapes.

Even though there were hip-hop supergroups prior to the late 2000s and the 2010s, the visibility they gained at the time was a sign of how far hip-hop had come. The emergence of new supergroups meant hip-hop had taken hold successfully, and for a long enough period

BAD MEETS EVIL DUO

Both hailing from Detroit, Michigan, Royce Da 5'9" and Eminem joined together as Bad Meets Evil in the late 1990s and early 2000s. During those years, they recorded a single for Eminem's debut album as well as underground songs and freestyles. The two produced well-received music together, but they parted ways in the early 2000s because of conflict between Royce Da 5'9" and members of Eminem's other group, D12. They reunited in 2011 to release two more singles and their first extended play, which hit the number one spot on the *Billboard* 200 charts.

Eminem and Royce Da 5'9" perform together as Bad Meets Evil in 1999.

of time so artists could shape their careers in different ways. Artists could enjoy achievements independently and then experiment with their music by working in a supergroup. Those supergroups didn't always reach the goals members may have once envisioned or that audiences would have liked to see. However, sometimes those groups exceeded expectations, giving their members a chance to grow as performers and expand the art of hip-hop.

> "We all had this box that everybody was putting us in. . . . The different flows and different styles automatically just came off the different beats. We all just attacked [the music] like we would attack our own . . . and it came out sounding like that."[2]
>
> —Royce Da 5'9"

8 FUTURE OF HIP-HOP
GROUPS

The group dynamic has been an important cornerstone of hip-hop. Since its beginning, hip-hop has been an interactive art form, marked by sampling, collaborating, and incorporating musical influences. Furthermore, hip-hop artists have often relied on the energy and accompaniment of their peers to achieve their creative goals. As a result, the noticeable presence of supergroups in the late 2000s and early 2010s has raised questions about this interactive tradition and what hip-hop groups will look like in the future.

Some music industry professionals believe traditional hip-hop groups are a thing of the past. In their view, artists will chart their own

Questlove of the Roots believes in the hip-hop group dynamic.

careers, sometimes forming supergroups for short-term projects but shying away from more permanent group memberships. To some, this is a negative trend that leads hip-hop away from its roots. To others, it is a natural step in the ever-evolving world of hip-hop.

Breaking with Tradition

Unique combinations of call-and-response, emceeing, deejaying, and vocal shifts between various rappers have distinguished hip-hop from other forms of music. Critics fear some of those features will be lost as solo artists dominate records. Questlove (Ahmir Khalib Thompson), a member of the decades-old group the Roots, shares this feeling. He also emphasizes that groups build community and a sense of shared purpose in life. In his perspective, even the inevitable problems in groups—disagreements, jealousy, rivalry—are valuable because they push

THE PAST IN THE PRESENT

Some of the groups from the past remain active. A Tribe Called Quest, for instance, released a new album in November 2016. *We Got It from Here . . . Thank You 4 Your Service* is the group's first new album in 18 years, during which time the band occasionally performed but mostly remained split over differences. However, group member Phife Dawg died of diabetes complications during the album's production, meaning the album will likely be the group's last.

artists to open their minds, view the world through others' eyes, and resolve disagreements. For Questlove and those who share his view, the "dying" of hip-hop groups means the loss of a complex and interactive creative process. In addition, it means a major change in the way hip-hop has looked and sounded in previous decades.[1]

Evolving Tradition

There are other industry professionals who hold a different view about the disappearance of groups. These professionals argue the decline of traditionally formed groups is a natural progression and another phase of hip-hop's development. At the same time, maintaining group harmony has sometimes been difficult and limiting.

FINANCIAL MOTIVATION

Questlove also suggests one possible reason for the decline of hip-hop groups may be financial motivation. It is often faster and more profitable for record labels to produce work by individual artists because there are fewer people involved. For that same reason, solo albums tend to have more financial incentive for the artist as well.

THE
ROOTS

Many hip-hop groups are closely connected to certain time periods or regions. The Roots stand out as a group that has spanned both time and region, adapting since the late 1980s to secure a place as one of hip-hop's most versatile and longest-standing groups. The Roots got their start when two core members, Black Thought (Tariq Trotter) and Questlove, began performing on the streets of Philadelphia. Only teenagers at the time, they freestyled to beats played on makeshift drums. Since then, they have maintained a unique, down-to-earth artistic appeal even as they've attained success.

Their successes include major record deals, platinum status, and a permanent spot as the chosen house band for Jimmy Fallon's television shows, *Late Night* and *The Tonight Show*. That 2009 choice marked a significant moment for hip-hop groups. Not only had they gained a place in the mainstream music industry, but now a hip-hop group was welcomed into US homes, appearing on millions of television screens night after night.

Members of the Roots are active in *The Tonight Show*, developing catchy sets with politicians, celebrities, and other musicians.

The more people involved in a song, the more difficult the production process becomes. Another concern is that groups can fall into creative ruts. Several prominent groups have taken breaks, allowing their members to pursue solo projects to remain fresh and broaden fan bases. The Wu-Tang Clan followed this model, contributing to its success. Artists in the future may continue looking for innovative ways to meld collaboration and solo pursuits. Opting for a range of short-term collaborations instead of long-term work with one group could allow artists to gather distinct experiences to shape their music.

THE FLEXIBLE STRUCTURE OF THE WU-TANG CLAN

Wu-Tang leader RZA encouraged his fellow group members to play to their strengths in their solo work to connect with varied listener tastes in a focused way. For example, RZA noticed Raekwon and Ghostface Killah appealed more to the gangsta style, GZA seemed to be for intellectuals, and Method Man had a playful side attractive to younger audiences. RZA believed this strategy would draw wider audiences to the group as a whole.

While hip-hop groups haven't gone extinct in the 2010s, the ways they are formed and the ways they operate have been changing. Traditionally formed groups no longer occupy the high-profile place they once did.

Instead, supergroups and solo performers often receive more attention. Attitudes vary about the changing role and makeup of groups, some viewing those changes as a loss of tradition and others viewing them as a normal evolution of an art form. At the very least, this debate over the future of groups shows how strongly the industry feels about the contribution groups have made in advancing hip-hop throughout history.

NEW HIP-HOP IN NEW YORK

New groups continue to form, drawing from history but also bringing new layers to the hip-hop scene. For example, Ratking, a four-member group of rappers and producers, broke onto the hip-hop scene in 2012 with its extended play *Wiki93*. It received high praise from music reviewers for its use of 1990s influences, its knack for New York storytelling, and its respect for hip-hop as a true art.

TIMELINE

1979

In October, the Sugarhill Gang releases "Rapper's Delight."

1983

Run-D.M.C. debuts its first single, "It's Like That."

1986

The Beastie Boys releases its first album, *Licensed to III*; Salt-N-Pepa puts out its debut, *Hot, Cool, & Vicious*.

1988

N.W.A draws attention to the West Coast with the release of *Straight Outta Compton*.

1990

A Tribe Called Quest emphasizes an Afrocentric philosophy as its first album, *People's Instinctive Travels and the Paths of Rhythm*, comes out.

1991

Cypress Hill releases its self-titled debut, which includes Spanish/English mixes, such as "Latin Lingo."

1992

The Wu-Tang Clan forms as one of the largest hip-hop groups and one with a unique business model.

1995

Tha Dogg Pound stirs concerns over dangerous gangsta hip-hop content with its debut, *Dogg Food*; Goodie Mob attracts the industry to "Dirty South" hip-hop with *Soul Food*.

1997

Bone Thugs-N-Harmony wins a Grammy for its hit "Crossroads."

1999

In February, TLC drops *FanMail*, the group's third hit album.

2004

Southern hip-hop group Outkast wins its sixth Grammy Award.

2007

Grandmaster Flash and the Furious Five becomes the first rap group to be inducted into the Rock & Roll Hall of Fame.

2009

In March, the Roots sign on as the house band for Jimmy Fallon's late-night television show.

2011

Supergroup CRS unveils its single "Don't Stop!" but never releases its anticipated full-length album.

2016

A Tribe Called Quest releases *We Got It from Here . . . Thank You 4 Your Service*, the group's first new album in 18 years.

ESSENTIAL
FACTS

KEY PLAYERS

- Grandmaster Flash and the Furious Five established socially conscious lyrics as a hip-hop staple through their song "The Message."

- N.W.A attracted attention to the West Coast and to controversial gangsta rap hip-hop and also propelled the careers of many industry legends, including Dr. Dre, Eazy-E, and Ice Cube.

- Salt-N-Pepa served as a trailblazing female trio, pushing back against a male-dominated hip-hop culture that objectified and mistreated women.

- Outkast established the South as an important hip-hop center while also leading hip-hop nationwide into the twenty-first century.

TRENDS

- Late 1970s: Pioneering groups transform the live art of hip-hop to recorded songs.

- 1980s: Groups highlight the importance of socially conscious messages in hip-hop.

- 1990s: Various groups usher in gender, geographic, and racial diversity.

- 2000s: Groups enjoy mainstream success, spanning the country in region and style.

- 2010s: Debates on the future occur as traditional groups seem to decline.

LEGACY

Hip-hop groups embody the interactive, collaborative, dynamic spirit of hip-hop. The group structure has given many artists the support they need to develop their skills and innovate new styles. While groups have been important in launching solo careers, they are also points of return. Artists who enjoy success independently often return to groups, even if just for a short window of time, to inspire their creativity.

QUOTE

"Groups lend texture, diversity, and distinct personalities to a track that individuals can't provide."

—*music writer Jeff Benjamin*

GLOSSARY

AFROCENTRIC
Focused in positive ways on Africa and the black community worldwide.

AUTHENTICITY
Having a true, real, and genuine quality.

BICOASTAL
Relating to two coasts.

CALL-AND-RESPONSE
When one artist delivers a song line and a second artist or the audience answers back.

DISS
Short for *disrespect*; to criticize someone or something.

EXTENDED PLAY
A musical recording of several songs, longer than a single but shorter than an album.

HARDCORE
Music that strongly expresses anger in the words and sound.

JIM CROW LAWS
State and local laws passed in the 1880s in the South to racially segregate blacks.

MATERIALISTIC
Focused on money and the things money can buy.

MINORITY

A person or group different from most others, usually because of race, religion, education level, or income.

MISOGYNY

Hatred of or contempt for women.

MIXTAPE

A compilation of unreleased tracks, freestyle rap music, and DJ mixes of songs.

SAMPLING

The process of using prerecorded sounds to create a new piece of music.

SCRATCHING

Moving a record back and forth under the needle to create a beat.

SOCIALLY CONSCIOUS

Having an awareness of the problems that certain groups of people face.

TURNTABLE

An electronic device consisting of a needle and a disk that spins. When the needle is placed on a vinyl record, it plays music.

ADDITIONAL
RESOURCES

SELECTED BIBLIOGRAPHY

Coleman, Brian. *Check the Technique: Liner Notes for Hip-Hop Junkies*. New York: Villard, 2007. Print.

Forman, Murray, and Mark Anthony Neal, editors. *That's the Joint!: The Hip-Hop Studies Reader*. New York: Routledge, 2004. Print.

Grem, Darren E. "'The South Got Something to Say:' Atlanta's Dirty South and the Southernization of Hip-Hop America." *Southern Cultures*, vol. 12, no. 4, Winter 2006, pp. 55–73. Print.

Hess, Mickey, ed. *Hip Hop in America: A Regional Guide*, vol. 1. Westport, CT: Greenwood, 2010. Print.

Peterson, James Braxton. *Hip-Hop Headphones: A Scholar's Critical Playlist*. New York: Bloomsbury, 2016. Print.

FURTHER READINGS

Baker, Soren. *The History of Rap and Hip-Hop*. Detroit, MI: Lucent, 2012. Print.

Cornish, Melanie. *The History of Hip Hop*. New York: Crabtree, 2009. Print.

Lusted, Marcia Amidon. *Hip-Hop Music*. Minneapolis: Abdo, 2017.

WEBSITES

To learn more about Hip-Hop Insider, visit **abdobooklinks.com**. These links are routinely monitored and updated to provide the most current information available.

FOR MORE INFORMATION

For more information on this subject, contact or visit the following organizations:

NATIONAL MUSEUM OF AFRICAN AMERICAN HISTORY AND CULTURE
1400 Constitution Ave NW
Washington, DC 20560
844-750-3012
https://nmaahc.si.edu
This museum holds a collection of photographs, artifacts, and accompanying information about iconic hip-hop artists and groups.

ROCK & ROLL HALL OF FAME
1100 Rock and Roll Boulevard
Cleveland, Ohio 44114
216-781-7625
https://www.rockhall.com
The Rock & Roll Hall of Fame honors artists from many genres, including hip-hop, who have made an important, lasting contribution to music.

UNIVERSAL HIP HOP MUSEUM
555 Bergen Avenue 3rd Floor
Bronx, New York 10452
347-454-2793
http://www.uhhm.org/
The Universal Hip Hop Museum is dedicated to sharing the history and culture of hip-hop with people of all ages. It offers virtual exhibits, public events, and educational and social programs.

SOURCE NOTES

CHAPTER 1. HIP-HOP IN THE HALL OF FAME

1. "Grandmaster Flash and the Furious Five accept and perform Rock Hall Inductions 2007." *YouTube*. YouTube, 23 Sept. 2011. Web. 17 Nov. 2016.

2. "Jay Z Inducts Grandmaster Flash and the Furious Five Rock Hall Inductions 2007." *YouTube*. YouTube, 23 Sept. 2011. Web. 17 Nov. 2016.

3. "Induction Process." *Rock & Roll Hall of Fame*. Rock & Roll Hall of Fame, n.d. Web. 19 Nov. 2016.

4. Mark Richardson. "Grandmaster Flash / Grandmaster Flash & the Furious Five: The Message." *Pitchfork*. Pitchfork, 14 July 2005. Web. 16 Nov. 2016.

5. Kendra A. King. *African American Politics*. Malden, MA: Polity Press, 2010. Print. 190.

6. "Jay Z Inducts Grandmaster Flash and the Furious Five Rock Hall Inductions 2007." *YouTube*. YouTube, 23 Sept. 2011. Web. 17 Nov. 2016.

CHAPTER 2. PIONEERING GROUPS

1. James Braxton Peterson. *Hip-Hop Headphones: A Scholar's Critical Playlist*. London: Bloomsbury, 2016. Print. 16.

2. "1983: Run DMC." University of Colorado at Boulder, n.d. Web. 22 Dec. 2016.

CHAPTER 3. DIVERSIFYING HIP-HOP

1. Jerico Mandybur. "Salt-N-Pepa on Women in Hip-Hop, Ferguson, MO, and Their Legacy." *Oyster*. Oyster, 20 Oct. 2014. Web. 17 Nov. 2016.

CHAPTER 4. WEST COAST HIP-HOP

1. Victoria Hernandez. "N.W.A.'s 'Straight Outta Compton' Certified Triple Platinum." *HipHopDX*. HipHopDX, 8 Dec. 2015. Web. 12 Nov. 2016.

2. Pancho McFarland. "Chicano Rap Roots: Black-Brown Cultural Exchange and the Making of a Genre." *Callaloo* 29.3 (2006): 950.

3. Toshitaka Kondo. "20 Years Later: B-Real & Sen Dog Talk Cypress Hill's 1991 Debut." *Complex*. Complex Media, 15 Aug. 2011. Web. 11 Nov. 2016.

4. Dave Wielenga. "In the Dogg House." *Rolling Stone* 720.2 (Nov. 1995).

5. Mark Anthony Neal. *That's the Joint!: The Hip-Hop Studies Reader*. New York: Routledge, 2004. Print. 58.

SOURCE NOTES
CONTINUED

CHAPTER 5. EAST COAST GROUPS

1. "'We Didn't Wanna Be Anybody Else': A Tribe Called Quest Reflects on Its Debut." *NRP Music*. NRP, 13 Nov. 2015. Web. 8 Nov. 2016.

2. Frannie Kelley. "The Wu-Tang Clan's 20-Year Plan." *NPR Music*. NPR, 8 Apr. 2013. Web. 20 Nov. 2016.

3. Amy L Chasteen and Thomas Shriver. "Rap and Resistance: A Social Movement Analysis of the Wu-Tang Clan." *Challenge: A Journal of Research on African American Men* 9.2 (1998): 6.

4. S. H. Fernando, Jr. "Mobb Deep Deliver 'Hell on Earth' to the Faithful." *Rolling Stone* 749.12 (Dec. 1996).

5. "Prodigy of Mobb Depp Talking About Hip-hop in Queensbridge." *YouTube*. YouTube, 5 Dec. 2015. Web. 17 Nov. 2016.

6. Ibid.

CHAPTER 6. MIDWEST AND SOUTH GROUPS

1. Mickey Hess, ed. *Hip Hop in America: A Regional Guide*. Santa Barbara, CA: Greenwood, 2010. Print. xxii.

2. Adam Bradley and Andrew DuBois, eds. *The Anthology of Rap*. New Haven, CT: Yale UP, 2010. Print.

CHAPTER 7. SUPERGROUPS OF HIP-HOP
1. "Lupe Fiasco Talks C.R.S. Album with Kanye, Pharrell." *Baller Status.* Baller Status, 12 June 2014. Web. 30 Nov. 2016.
2. Andres Tardio. "Slaughterhouse: Rap in the Key of Life." *HipHopDX.* HipHopDX, 12 Aug. 2009. Web. 30 Nov. 2016.

CHAPTER 8. FUTURE OF HIP-HOP GROUPS
1. Ahmir "Questlove" Thompson and Ben Greenman. *Mo' Meta Blues: The World According to Questlove.* New York: Grand Central Publishing, 2013. Print. 4.
2. Jeff Benjamin. "Hip-Hop's Mightiest Supergroups." *Fuse.* Fuse, 26 June 2013. Web. 30 Nov. 2016.

INDEX

ABOUT THE AUTHOR

Rebecca Morris has a PhD in English from Texas A&M University. She is coeditor of *Representing Children in Chinese and U.S. Children's Literature* (Ashgate, 2014) and a contributor to *Jacqueline Wilson* (ed. Lucy Pearson, Palgrave Macmillan New Casebooks, 2015). In addition to writing nonfiction books, Morris also writes for several educational websites.